THIS BITES

A FIELD GUIDE TO MONSTER DEFENSE

by Tweedy Britches

Copyright © 2019 by Kissing Frog Books, LLC

Cover design by ktarrier at SelfPubBookCovers.com

All rights reserved. No part of this book may be reproduced or transmitted in any form or by any means without prior written permission of the author, except where permitted by law. Please respect the hard work of this author by purchasing and reading only legal, authorized copies of this book.

Names, characters, and incidents are the products of the author's imagination or are used fictionally. Any similarity to actual events, locations, or people, living or dead, is coincidental.

This book is dedicated to the creepy,
crawly, mysterious creatures
that go bump in the night.
They help make life interesting.

Acknowledgements

This book and I have been on quite a journey together. We survived an economic collapse, loads of rejections, two literary agents, a contest win, the creation of a publishing company, a long-distance move, and finally, publication. I'm exhausted just thinking about it.

Despite the challenges, this book and I stuck together, and now the world will be a safer place.

Thanks to my endlessly supportive friends and family whose names I won't mention, lest a monster reads this and goes searching for fresh snacks. Thanks especially to my outstanding writing group! You know who you are. You guys are a blast!

Finally, thanks to everyone who reads this book. My favorite part of being an author is that there are people who could be thinking unpleasant thoughts about things like politics or snowstorms or where that gross smell is coming from, but instead, they're laughing about monsters. Cool, huh?

Table of Contents

Chapter 1 – Introduction 1
    Activity 1.1: Monster Identification Quiz 8

Chapter 2 – Vampires 9
    Recognizing vampires 9
        Activity 2.1: Are You a Vampire? 11
        Activity 2.2: Vampire Identification Quiz 14
    Avoiding vampires 15
        Activity 2.3: Count the Vampires 17
    Repelling vampires 18
    Caught by a vampire 20
        Activity 2.4: Un-Welcome Mat 23
        Activity 2.5: Anti-Vampire Weapon 25
    Becoming a vampire 26

Chapter 3 – Zombies 27
    Recognizing zombies 28
        Activity 3.1: Who's Most Dangerous? 31
    Avoiding zombies 32
        Activity 3.2: Stay Awake! 35
    Repelling zombies 36

Caught by a zombie 37

    Activity 3.3: Anti-Zombie Weapons 41

Becoming a zombie 43

    Activity 3.4: Zombie Job Application 45

Chapter 4 – Werewolves 47

Recognizing werewolves 48

    Activity 4.1: Phases of the Moon 50

Avoiding werewolves 52

    Activity 4.2: Woodland Hazards 55

Repelling werewolves 56

    Activity 4.3: Outcast Benefits 59

Caught by a werewolf 60

    Activity 4.4: Werewolf Escape Quiz 63

    Activity 4.5: Silver Items 66

Becoming a werewolf 67

Chapter 5 – Witches 71

Recognizing witches 72

Avoiding witches 79

    Activity 5.1: Fun with Witches 81

    Activity 5.2: Creepy Castle Pop Quiz 86

Activity 5.3: Witch Identification Test 89

Repelling witches 90

Activity 5.4: Learning from Rabbits 91

Caught by a witch.. 95

Activity 5.5: Beach-Going Witches 99

Becoming a witch.. 102

Conclusion... 105

Other titles from Kissing Frog Books

About the Author

Chapter 1

Introduction

You know that feeling on Halloween when you're out trick-or-treating, and you just want to do one more block before going home? There's still room in your bag for more candy, and the next row of houses all have their porch lights on. You're sure that every one of them is giving away full-sized chocolate bars. You should go home because it's getting late, but you keep walking.

You finish that block and see there's another block on the other side of the next street, then another after that. Before you know it, your bag is almost too heavy to carry, and the sky is pitch dark.

That's what happened to me when I was ten years old.

My friends had gone home already because their candy was in normal-sized pillowcases that filled up too soon. My pillowcase was for a king-size bed, so by the time it was full, I could barely lift it.

I was afraid of getting in trouble for staying out too late, so I decided to take a shortcut through the graveyard. As I passed through the cemetery gates, the clouds shifted and a bright full moon shone down on me. Somewhere in the distance, a dog howled.

No matter what anyone says, lugging a king-sized pillowcase full of chocolate is hard work, even if you are dressed like Superman. My heart was thudding, and the overstuffed sack of candy was thumping against my blue tights with each step. The thudding and the thumping grew louder, until they sounded more like pounding. That's when I realized the sound wasn't coming from me, but from someone running up behind me. And there was snarling—lots of angry snarling.

I was delighted to hear the newcomer. Here was someone to help me carry that massive pillowcase. With any luck, they wouldn't like chocolate so I wouldn't have to share, but even if I had to give up a piece or two, it would be a small price to pay. I pulled a tiny green sucker out of the sack and waved it over my head.

In those days, I was both young and brave. It was only time and experience that turned me into the mature twelve-year-old coward I am today. But back then I didn't understand the dangers that surrounded me at every turn. I couldn't imagine how anything would hurt me on a deserted cemetery road under a full moon on Halloween. So I stopped and stood, waving candy over my head like a fool.

A creature suddenly sprang from behind a tall headstone and crashed into me, its teeth and claws straining to sink into my throat. I panicked. I screamed. I tried to swing my massive pillowcase, but it was too heavy. That would have been the end of me, but the cemetery's gravediggers had been lazy that day and left an empty grave next to the road. I fell into the six-foot hole, and it saved my life.

Above me, a huge dark shape circled the hole, glaring down at me, snarling and howling in frustration. It was shaped like a large, muscular man, but sometimes it walked upright like a human and other times it stalked on all four feet like a wolf. Its head was wolf-shaped with a long snout and pointed ears. The creature's eyes glowed red in the darkness.

I cowered in terror at the bottom of that hole, convinced that at any moment, the creature would jump down and devour me. Worse, it might go for my candy first, then

I'd have to watch while all my lovely chocolate disappeared. I had never been more scared in my life, until something happened to make me more scared: Another creature joined the first!

Again, I could only see the shadow outlined against the sky at the top of the hole, but this creature was even bigger. It was also growling and snarling. Wolf slobber fell down into the hole and splattered on my head. It was disgusting. And terrifying. And unpleasantly moist.

It was clear that the two creatures were fighting over me. Or maybe over my candy. It was hard to say for sure. They began to bark and bite at each other as they circled the hole. Flecks of wolf blood splattered on me along with the slobber. That was even more disgusting, terrifying, and unpleasantly moist.

Shortly, another wolf creature showed up and began circling and fighting with the others. Then another. And another.

Eventually there were no fewer than a dozen man-wolf creatures milling around above. I was constantly afraid that with so many beasts crowding around, one would get pushed into the hole with me.

Finally, the sky overhead began to lighten. Dawn was breaking! That's when the man-wolves started to calm down. They stopped snarling, the shower of goo dried up, and they drifted away from the hole.

When the sky was fully bright and I hadn't heard any noise from the creatures in a while, I hoisted my bag over one shoulder and began climbing up. The bag was considerably lighter now since I had eaten a number of candy bars while I was stuck in the hole. They had helped keep up my strength and steady my nerves throughout a long night.

At the top, the scene was shocking. More than a dozen people in tattered clothes were fast asleep. They littered the grass the way discarded candy wrappers littered the bottom of the hole where I had been hiding. There were boys and girls, men and women, all covered in cuts and scrapes from fights the night before. They were filthy and muddy and smelled like they had been wrestling wet dogs all night.

That was my first encounter with monsters. I came to learn that the beasts in the cemetery were werewolves. If it hadn't been for that convenient six-foot hole, I would have been a goner that night. Or I would have been turned into a werewolf myself, which is worse because the smell of wet dog never comes out of your clothes.

IMPORTANT SAFETY TIP: Always have a deep hole nearby to hide in.

I'm Tweedy Britches, and I believe in monsters. I've met them up close, smelled their stinky breath, and chased them out of my bathtub. Monsters are real, and I have survived by knowing that these vile creatures are waiting in every closet, down every dark alley, and at the bottom of every extra-large popcorn bucket.

I might look like I'm only in sixth grade, but I've spent years researching how to protect myself. All that dangerous, exhausting, smelly research has now been put into this book where you, too, can use it to keep yourself safe.

Most people say that monsters don't exist. They say there's no reason to protect yourself from creatures like vampires, werewolves, and witches because they aren't real. Well, you can believe these so-called experts if you like, but I know they're wrong.

The "experts" might *hope* that flesh-eating fiends or spell-casting hags aren't walking down the streets outside their homes and schools, but how can they be sure? And what if those experts are telling you not to worry so *you* will be careless and become an easy victim for lurking creatures of the night? Meanwhile, they sit safe and secure in monster-free buildings.

> **IMPORTANT SAFETY TIP:** Never trust experts.

No, don't call me a monster expert; you can actually trust *my* advice. Instead, just think of me as a sensible person who prefers to keep his blood *inside* his body instead of dripping down a monster's fangs.

Whether you believe monsters are real or not, it never hurts to take precautions. If you wear smelly garlic around your neck every day, but never run into a vampire, there's no harm done. Except to your social life. Which will be sad and lonely.

On the other hand, if you find yourself facing a hungry bloodsucker and are completely unprepared, you will become dinner. So keep reading, and this book will help you cover your bases—even if those bases are littered with the evil undead.

ACTIVITY 1.1

Monster Identification Quiz

<u>Instructions</u>: Select which of the following is a dangerous creature that wants to turn you into monster kibble. Circle all that apply.

    A.   A bloodthirsty vampire
    B.   A brainless zombie
    C.   A hungry werewolf
    D.   An evil witch
    E.   Professor Knose I.T. All, Expert

<u>Answer:</u> *If you circled all of the above, congratulations! You are well on your way to learning the secrets of staying off the monster menu.*

Chapter 2
Vampires

The problem with vampires is that they are technically dead and must drink human blood to keep walking and talking like real, live people. Depending on who you listen to, a vampire might or might not be controlled by a demon spirit inside its body. From your point of view, it doesn't really matter if a demon is in there or not. The creature wants to drain the life from you and possibly turn you into a monster. Do you have to ask for its family history?

Recognizing Vampires
1. Not attractive: Hollywood movies want us to believe that vampires are beautiful people who can hypnotize others by looking deep into their eyes. This is untrue. The perfect-

looking actors who play vampires are not actually undead. That would be impossible because vampires can't have their pictures taken.

Hollywood wants us to think that vampires are attractive because many movie directors, producers, and writers are vampires. They just want to feel good about themselves.

IMPORTANT SAFETY TIP: Hollywood is full of cold-blooded monsters. And lots of vampires live there, too.

ACTIVITY 2.1
Are You a Vampire?

Vampires cannot see their own reflections in mirrors. Use the following test to figure out if you are already a vampire.

Instructions:

Step 1: Go into your bathroom and look in the mirror. If you see your reflection, then you are not a vampire. Congratulations! Don't get cocky, though; you might still be some other kind of monster. Keep reading to find out what kind.

Step 2: If you cannot see your reflection, then you are already a vampire. Or the light is off and the room is dark.

Step 3: If the light is off, turn it on and try the test again. If you still cannot see your reflection, then you are definitely a vampire. Skip to the last section of this chapter to figure out your next move.

Recognizing Vampires (continued)

2. <u>Teeth, eyes, skin, and wardrobe:</u> Vampires have glowing red eyes, which help them see in the dark. Their canine teeth are long and sharply pointed, and their skin is deathly pale. Unlike what many people think, they don't wear capes, and they can't turn into bats. In other words, don't bother searching for guys whose flowing capes might be hiding a set of wings. The only people you will find who look like that are not vampires. Most of them are art teachers.

> **IMPORTANT SAFETY TIP:** Art teachers rarely thirst for human blood.

3. <u>Strong:</u> Vampires are strong. Much stronger than normal humans. Your mother tells you that eating spinach will build your muscles, which might be true, but there isn't enough spinach in the world to make you as strong as a vampire. In fact, if you are always full of spinach, it will slow you down while you are trying to escape from bloodthirsty creatures of the night.

> **IMPORTANT SAFETY TIP:** Do not waste your time with spinach.

4. <u>Cold skin:</u> Since vampires are dead, they can't keep themselves warm like living humans do. Their skin is always the same temperature as the air around them. This doesn't bother them, though. They are just as comfortable in the 115 degree desert heat as in the 50 degrees below zero Antarctic winter. Although you will rarely find vampires in Antarctica or the desert. There aren't enough people to eat in these spots to make the long trip worthwhile.

One good way to identify a vampire is by looking at how he's dressed. Because their bodies don't heat or cool themselves, vampires pay little attention to the weather. If you see a person dressed too warmly—with long sleeves or boots or a parka—on a hot day, he is probably a vampire. If this person is dressed that way and not sweating, he is *definitely* a vampire.

> **IMPORTANT SAFETY TIP:** Anyone wearing flip-flops and shorts outdoors in winter is a vampire. Or a high school student. Either way, run!

ACTIVITY 2.2
Vampire Identification Quiz

<u>Instructions:</u> Circle which of the following is a vampire.

A. Man wearing swimming trunks, standing on an iceberg at night surrounded by penguins

> *Answer:* Definitely a vampire. Or just a nut who's about to freeze to death.

B. Man in a business suit sitting on a bus holding a briefcase

> *Answer:* Maybe a vampire. See the section "Avoiding vampires."

C. A pale woman lurking in an art museum wearing dark glasses and a cape

> *Answer:* Relax, she's an art teacher. However, she's probably about to break into an explanation of Post-Impressionism on modern art or something equally pointless, so run!

Avoiding vampires

The best way to protect yourself from a vampire attack is to never run into the monsters in the first place. If you are fairly sure that no vampires currently live in your house, then you are probably safe there.

Since you can have everything you need delivered to your home—from pizza and groceries to toothpaste and books—there's no reason to risk going out into the world. After all, thirsty vampires could be lurking just around the corner.

> **IMPORTANT SAFETY TIP:** Never leave your house.

If you insist on taking your life into your hands by going outside, then there are some places you could go that are more risky than others.

1. <u>School:</u> This is probably okay. It happens during the day when vampires are asleep. Remember that nighttime school activities like concerts and parent evenings are out of the question. All those families wandering around are like a restaurant for vampires. And everyone's blood is full of sugar from the punch and cookies that are always served at these events. Vampires can't resist sweet blood, so don't

risk it. Fake a stomachache and stay home.

2. <u>Malls:</u> *Never* go to an indoor mall for any reason! They have no windows, so even if it is daylight outside, vampires could still be wandering around the mall trying on pants and getting their ears pierced.

> **IMPORTANT SAFETY TIP:** A craving for Cinnabon could cost you your life.

3. <u>Amusement parks:</u> During the day when the sun is out, these are generally safe. But get out of there before nightfall. Vampires love meeting their undead friends, and riding some roller coasters, then snacking on a few kids who are too dizzy from the Tilt-a-Whirl to fight back.

> **IMPORTANT SAFETY TIP:** Carnivals do not attract vampires because even the undead are afraid of the so-called "carnies" who work at them. This does not mean carnivals are safe. If vampires fear them, you should, too.

ACTIVITY 2.3

Count the Vampires

<u>Instructions:</u> Next time you are at an amusement park, look around and consider how many vampires could be there if it were after sunset. How many do you see?

<u>Answer:</u> *There could be hundreds of possible vampires. What are you doing at such a dangerous place?*
- Everyone on the roller coaster is a vampire.
- There might be one hiding behind the trashcan and several more in the bathroom.
- The guy selling balloons is probably a vampire, and you don't want to know what he did with all the kids whose balloons he stole.
- The workers dressed in costumes of cartoon animals are definitely vampires. No human could stand the heat inside those fur suits. They can be out either day or night since the huge mouse masks protect them from the sun.

IMPORTANT SAFETY TIP: Never pose with a costumed cartoon animal. Vampire or not, those things are creepy.

Avoiding vampires (continued)

4. Grocery stores: These are all right at any time of day. Garlic in the produce department keeps vampires away. For the same reason, Italian restaurants are always safe, not to mention delicious.

5. Cemeteries: Are you kidding? If I even have to tell you to avoid cemeteries, then you have not been paying attention at all. When vampires aren't lurking in malls or attacking kids who have just gotten off the amusement park's Spinning Octopus, they are hiding out in cemeteries. They feel comfortable around the dead, and a lot of their friends are buried there. Why would anyone in his right mind go *looking* for vampire hangouts?

Repelling vampires

If you happen to stumble into a spot where there might be vampires, there are a few ways to keep them from looking at you for their next meal.

1. Garlic: You can try stringing a bunch of garlic cloves together and wearing it around your neck. Vampires do not like the smell (join the club), so they will avoid you. They would rather snack on someone less stinky.

> **IMPORTANT SAFETY TIP:** Beware of anyone who wears garlic. They want the vampire to eat you first.

Keep in mind that if you insist on walking around wearing a necklace of garlic, people will stop returning your phone calls. It would probably be easier to make friends if you actually *were* a moving corpse with glowing red eyes. But if you find that you have too many party invitations and need a plan to reduce your popularity at school, this is the way to go.

2. <u>Crosses:</u> You can wear a cross around your neck, and it will repel vampires. Unlike garlic, a cross doesn't have any bad odor and it can be tucked into your shirt until a bloodsucker makes a dive for your throat.

The downside of crosses is that they have to be seen or touched by the vampire in order to work. If you have one stuffed deep in your pocket, it will not do you any good. Just to be on the safe side, you might want to have a cross tattooed over the artery on your throat. Your mom might think it is extreme, but see who has the last laugh next time your family is on a camping trip in Transylvania.

> **IMPORTANT SAFETY TIP:** Never camp in Transylvania.

3. <u>Holy water:</u> This is water that has been blessed by a priest. It is a great thing to have because it's easy to carry, and if you spill it on a vampire, it burns him. It can even be kept in a handy spray bottle for when you are dealing with a lot of vampires at once.

The big problem here is getting your hands on some. You can find holy water at Catholic churches, but you are not allowed to take it. And if you ask a priest to bless water for you, he is sure to ask why. A priest will definitely be one of those "experts" who says there is no such thing as vampires.

> **IMPORTANT SAFETY TIP:** Your mother will not be happy if a priest tells her you asked for five gallons of holy water.

Caught by a vampire

If you foolishly leave the house without garlic, crosses, or a jug of holy water, then you will probably be caught by a vampire. Even if you take all possible precautions, you still have a strong chance of running into a hungry bloodsucker some day. Especially if you ride the bus. Since vampires cannot have their pictures taken, they cannot get driver's licenses. That means they have to ride the bus. At least half of the people you see on the bus after dark are vampires. They often carry briefcases to blend in with people coming home from work.

> **IMPORTANT SAFETY TIP:** You do *not* want to know what vampires carry in their briefcases. Trust me on this.

1. <u>Try to escape:</u> If a vampire is chasing you, do not climb a tree. This could be very dangerous because vampires are much better climbers than you are. No, wait, that's wrong. I'm thinking of bears.

> **IMPORTANT SAFETY TIP:** Vampires are not bears.

If a vampire is chasing you, then you could go up a tree, but what if a bear is already up there? You are better off ducking into a church where the vampire cannot follow. (This will usually work with bears, too). Then you just relax in church and wait for sunrise. When the sun comes up, you can come outside and the vampire will be gone. Be careful, though, because the bear might still be hanging around waiting for you.

If there is no church handy, you can try running into your house or a friend's house. A vampire cannot enter a home unless he has been invited by the owner. This means that you are safe inside a house as long as no fool has issued an invitation to the vampire. By the way, a mat on the front step that reads "Welcome" could be considered an invitation by a hungry vampire.

> **IMPORTANT SAFETY TIP:** Never invite anyone into your house.

You might think that never letting another person into your house is being too careful. After all, you can usually spot vampires by their glowing red eyes, long teeth, and pale skin. You might think it is easy to avoid letting people in who look like this, while only opening the door for your mother or the pizza delivery guy.

But what if a vampire is disguised as a high school student delivering a pizza? He could wear sunglasses to hide his eyes, put on braces to hide his weird teeth, and have pale skin from playing video games indoors every day. Don't be fooled.

ACTIVITY 2.4
Un-Welcome Mat

Vampires cannot enter your home unless you invite them. Unfortunately, a welcome mat on the porch is just the invitation they're looking for. Protect yourself by putting a new message in front of your door.

<u>Instructions:</u> Trace or copy the picture below on a separate sheet of paper. Feel free to use the back of your sister's book report that's due tomorrow. She'll thank you someday when she's not eaten by a vampire. After she gets out of detention for not doing her homework, that is. Then simply place the picture outside your front door.

NOT WELCOME!

Caught by a vampire (continued)

2. <u>Killing vampires:</u> If it turns out that you cannot escape from the vampire, then your only choice is to kill the creature. Just remember this simple rule: Whatever kills humans usually kills vampires. No, wait, I'm thinking of bears again. Vampires are a completely different challenge.

Vampires can be killed in one of several ways. First, you can thrust a wooden stake or other object made out of wood (sharpened pencil, coffee table, oak tree, etc.) into their hearts. The thing that makes this really difficult is that vampires tend not to stand still while you are trying to kill them. In fact, they usually fight back and try to bite you.

You can also kill a vampire by cutting off its head. You will need something sharp to do the job, like an ax or one of those foil yogurt lids. But, again, the vampire will fight back and he might have a yogurt lid of his own.

> **IMPORTANT SAFETY TIP:** Yogurt can be your best friend or your worst enemy.

Finally, vampires burn. But they don't want to. If a vampire blows out your match, you have a serious problem.

ACTIVITY 2.5
Anti-Vampire Weapon

Instructions: Find your little brother and take away the Popsicle he is eating. If he complains, explain that he'll thank you some day when you save him from a bloodthirsty vampire.

Finish eating the Popsicle, then rinse off the wooden stick and stow it in your pocket. Keep this weapon on your person at all times.

In case of vampire emergency, simply drive the piece of wood into the monster's heart. The heart is on the upper left side of his chest. Aim carefully. If you miss and get his spleen or big toe instead, the vampire is not going to return your stick and give you a second shot.

Becoming a vampire

Sorry if this book failed to keep you safe from vampires. We tried, right? But as long as you are a powerful supernatural creature now, you should make the best of it. How about using your incredible strength to settle some scores?

Remember the kid who stole your windbreaker on the playground that time, then your mom yelled at you for losing it? Wouldn't he make a nice meal? And what about the girl who came to your birthday party in kindergarten but didn't bring a gift? Yum. And you just know that the lunch lady at school secretly *enjoys* serving kids stuffed green peppers. She better start wearing a garlic necklace.

> **IMPORTANT SAFETY TIP:** Do not make enemies of people who might become vampires some day.

Chapter 3
Zombies

Zombies get no respect because they are slow and stupid. But since they are rotting corpses, they should get credit for moving and thinking at all.

Some people believe that each zombie is controlled by an evil sorcerer. They think the sorcerer has a mission for his zombie to carry out, and the creature will keep moving until it has completed its task. If that is true, it might be good news because it means the zombie probably is not looking for you. It is simply following its master's orders and will ignore everyone as long as they stay out of its way. On the other hand, if the sorcerer has sent the zombie after *you* for some reason, then that spells trouble.

> **IMPORTANT SAFETY TIP:** Do not get evil sorcerers mad at you.

There are others who believe zombies are not controlled by anyone. They are just dead bodies that have come back to life for some reason and must eat human flesh in order to survive. They pose a real danger because A) they might eat you and B) even if they only take a small nibble before you escape, you will turn into a zombie.

As in the case of vampires that might be controlled by a demon, it doesn't matter whether zombies are controlled by a sorcerer or not. It is only important to know that zombies are always hungry and they can turn you into an evil, flesh-eating monster.

> **IMPORTANT SAFETY TIP:** Do not get turned into an evil, flesh-eating monster.

Recognizing zombies

1. <u>Slow and stupid:</u> Zombies move slowly with blank expressions on their faces. You might mistake your parents for zombies first thing in the morning. If you have a teenage brother, he could easily be mistaken for a zombie any

time of the day.

If you want to make sure a person is really a zombie and not a normal human who has just woken up (or a teenager), there is a simple test. Yell, "Look, it's a zombie!" If the person perks up and glances around to see where you are pointing, then he is not a zombie. If he does not react, then he is probably undead.

> **IMPORTANT SAFETY TIP:** Zombies do not surprise easily.

2. <u>Poor hygiene:</u> Zombies are covered with dirt and their tattered clothes hang off of them. Again, they can be mistaken for teenagers, but zombies don't wear their pants so low. Zombies are coated with dirt because they crawled out of graves. No one knows what the teenagers' excuse is, although some experts believe they are using the dirt as camouflage to hide a new tattoo from their mother.

As always, you can yell, "Look, it's a zombie!" to test whether a suspicious person is, in fact, a walking corpse. A zombie will not react at all, while a teenager is likely to snarl, "So what?"

3. <u>Rotten flesh:</u> When zombies reach out to grab you, you

will notice that their flesh is rotting right off their bones. And sometimes their bones are not connected too well, either. If you are unfortunate enough to touch one, you will notice that, like vampires, their skin is always room temperature. It's all part of the trouble with being a corpse. If zombies do not eat a lot of human flesh, they will keep rotting until they fall apart completely. The least rotted ones are those that catch the most food.

IMPORTANT SAFETY TIP: The best-looking zombies are the most dangerous.

ACTIVITY 3.1

Who's Most Dangerous?

<u>Instructions:</u> Based on what you have learned so far, select which of the following represents the greatest threat to a person's health and safety:

A. A zombie
B. A teenager
C. The teenager's mother

<u>Answer</u>: *If you chose the teenager's mother, you are correct. She becomes the most dangerous creature on earth when she sees that her child has gotten a tattoo.*

Recognizing zombies (continued)

4. <u>Bad breath:</u> Zombies always have bad breath. And I mean *really* bad. Their flesh is rotting, which creates a powerful stink all by itself. Plus, they are known for having poor brushing habits, and they eat nothing but raw people. You do the math.

Just because you meet someone who has bad breath, that does not mean he is a zombie. People living in your very own home could wake up and be slow and stupid first thing in the morning. Then they stumble around with bad breath until they get their turn in the bathroom. It does not mean they are all zombies. There is a slim chance they are not. Try the "Look, it's a zombie!" trick on them to make sure.

IMPORTANT SAFETY TIP: The "Look, it's a zombie!" trick will not work on your grandfather unless he is wearing his hearing aid.

Avoiding zombies

When you are trying to stay away from zombies, it is always a good idea to avoid going to places where zombies are likely to be found. The following list will give you some ideas of dangerous and not-so-dangerous zombie spots.

1. <u>Cemeteries:</u> Duh! Where do you think zombies come from in the first place? This is like a hotel for the dead! And many zombies are so stupid that they cannot find their way out of the cemetery once they dig themselves up. They just shuffle around, bumping into gravestones, and knocking over the nice vases of flowers that people left for their loved ones. Don't even think about visiting cemeteries.

2. <u>Funeral homes:</u> Double Duh! See #1 above. These are even worse than cemeteries because funeral homes usually serve coffee and cookies. People cannot run away from zombies as quickly when they are carrying cups and munching on treats.

> **IMPORTANT SAFETY TIP:** Zombies have the advantage when people are distracted by snacks.

3. <u>Your bedroom:</u> You probably think that your room is pretty safe from zombies, but you are wrong. Your bedroom has your bed in it. You go in there, lie down, close your eyes, and fall asleep. Zombies are slow, but even they can catch up to someone who is sleeping. That makes bedrooms extremely dangerous for those trying to stay away

from zombies.

> **IMPORTANT SAFETY TIP:** Never fall asleep.

ACTIVITY 3.2
Stay Awake!

<u>Instructions:</u> Next time you are thinking about falling asleep, consider what could happen if a zombie were to get into your house when you are not awake. Trace a copy of the picture below and tape it to the ceiling over your bed. It will remind you of the danger and prevent any ill-advised napping. Use crayons or markers to make it especially terrifying. A green-faced zombie will keep anyone awake.

Avoiding zombies (continued)

4. <u>The "10 Items or Less" aisle at the grocery store:</u> Zombies move very slowly, so they like to be around people who are just as slow as they are. That makes it easier for them to catch up with their prey. They know that nothing moves slower than the "fast" aisle at the grocery store where you aren't allowed to have more than 10 items in your cart. Even though I said you are safe from vampires at the grocery store, you still need to watch out for zombies.

> IMPORTANT SAFETY TIP: Never shop for groceries.

5. <u>The bus:</u> This is a safe place to be if you are worried about zombies. Those monsters are too stupid to count out the correct fare and too slow to run for the bus as it pulls away. Unfortunately, as you know, buses are (literally) crawling with vampires. Decide for yourself whether it is worth the risk.

Repelling zombies

These creatures are only interested in you if you are a living, breathing human whose flesh they can eat. That means you can easily become less delicious by making one of the following simple changes in your lifestyle.

1. <u>Stop living:</u> If you stop being alive, zombies will lose interest in you. If you are no longer alive, you can become any number of other things, including a zombie or a vampire. Take your pick.

2. <u>Stop breathing:</u> If you stop breathing for too long, it will lead to #1 above. The benefit of this tactic is that zombies will no longer want to eat you.

3. <u>Stop being human:</u> As with option #1 above, if you take this route, you can choose to become a vampire or a zombie. For a change of pace, you could also turn into a werewolf, a mummy, or a ghost. They, too, are safe from zombies.

> **IMPORTANT SAFETY TIP:** Zombies will not bite werewolves because that would turn them into werewolf-zombies. Some call them *wombies*. Even zombies are not stupid enough to want that.

Caught by a zombie

Sometimes even the best of us find ourselves in the clutches of a stinking, rotting member of the walking undead. Follow these simple steps to save yourself.

1. <u>Try to escape:</u> If you were moving so slowly that a zombie caught you, then you must really have a problem.

> **IMPORTANT SAFETY TIP:** Move faster!

Okay, let's say that you did not follow my advice and accidentally fell asleep. When you woke up, you were staring into the bulging eyes of a zombie. First, you need to push the monster away, giving you time to run.

As you are dashing out of your house in terror, you might want to shout to your family that there is a hungry zombie roaming around. If you warn them of the danger, they cannot blame you if they find themselves eaten by the creature. You do not need to slow down to alert them—it is better to keep moving. The smartest and quickest members of your family will probably get the message.

> **IMPORTANT SAFETY TIP:** It is polite to warn others when they are about to be eaten. On the other hand, if a zombie devours your teenage brother, it will not be as hungry for you.

2. <u>Fight back:</u> If you are walking down the street and happen to spot a zombie, don't worry. It will usually dart into a

small hole in the ground and hope that you're too big to follow. It will not leave its hole until you are long gone. No, wait, that's wrong. I'm thinking of chipmunks. Zombies do not care if you see them.

If a zombie sees you, he will follow. Fortunately, zombies are slow, so it is usually easy to get away. But sometimes you find yourself surrounded by a herd of zombies. In that case, you have to fight them. Since their flesh is rotting, you might be able to pull off an arm here or there and use it as a weapon against the others. If one of them falls over, grabbing a leg and swinging that around is even better.

3. <u>Kill the zombie:</u> If you cannot get away from a zombie, you might have to kill it. Well, since it is already dead, you do not have to "kill" it. You just have to make it stop moving. One way to do this is to cut off its head. Since they are slow and their bodies are falling apart anyway, it is not hard to cut off a zombie's head. You just need a sharp object to do the cutting. An ax works very well. A long strand of dental floss can work, but you really need to know what you're doing.

IMPORTANT SAFETY TIP: Cinnamon flavored dental floss is especially deadly.

ACTIVITY 3.3

Anti-Zombie Weapons

<u>Instructions</u>: Select which of the following is the best weapon to use against zombies.

A. Dental floss
B. An axe
C. Yogurt lid
D. A hawk

<u>Answer:</u> *All of the above can be effective. The hawk is best if you don't want to get zombie guts on your hands. The bird will swoop in, grip the undead creature in its talons, and carry it into the woods to eat it. No, wait, that's chipmunks again.*

Caught by a zombie (continued)

If you are dealing with a zombie that is being controlled by an evil sorcerer, you could kill the monster by making the sorcerer leave you alone. That might be easy or hard, depending on why the sorcerer is after you in the first place. For example, maybe the sorcerer sent his zombie after you because he was mad about not getting an invitation to your birthday party. If that is the case, then you can apologize to the sorcerer and maybe bring him a nice gift to make him feel better.

IMPORTANT SAFETY TIP: Evil sorcerers respond well to fruit baskets.

On the other hand, if the sorcerer wanted his zombie to catch you so he could use your brain in a horrible experiment, then you probably need more than a fruit basket. Perhaps you could suggest he use someone else's brain instead.

IMPORTANT SAFETY TIP: You might have a cousin who rarely uses his brain and would never notice if it were missing.

Becoming a zombie

If you move slowly or sleep or eat or buy groceries, then you will probably be bitten by a zombie. After that first bite, you might escape, but you will still turn into a zombie. It really is a shame, because after only one little nibble, you are a monster forever.

Don't be too upset if this happens to you. Even zombies can lead meaningful lives. Well, not "lives" exactly, because they aren't really alive. You know what I mean. You'll just need to find a job where you don't have to move too fast.

Working as the check-out person in the supermarket's "10 Items or Less" line would be a good career choice for a zombie. Or, if groceries aren't your thing, you might consider making ice cream cones for people visiting the zoo.

No other humans on the planet move as slowly as the zoo's ice cream cone makers. Have you ever seen how long the line is for that ice cream? It starts across from the polar bears, goes straight through the children's zoo, and comes out by the dolphins. That line spans three oceans and four continents. And this is not simply because everyone at the zoo wants ice cream. It is because the people scooping ice cream behind the counter think the zoo's sloths are too hyper. They believe the sloths need to relax and slow down a bit.

> **IMPORTANT SAFETY TIP:** Zombies and sloths have a lot in common.

Finally, if you are a zombie, you will need to feast on human flesh, but you can be polite about it. Remember to use a napkin when you are finished. You might *be* a monster but you do not have to *act* like one.

ACTIVITY 3.4
Zombie Job Application

<u>Instructions</u>: To get a job as a "10 Items or Less" cashier, simply fill out the application on the next page and return it to your local grocery store. You must make a good impression to get the job, so wear your best set of tattered, mud-stained rags to the interview.

During an interview, you might be asked "Why would you make a good employee?" A human might respond that he or she is "a people-person," which means that he or she enjoys spending time with other people. A zombie should *not* say that he or she is "a people-*eating* person."

Job Application for "10 Items or Less" Cashier

1. Name _____

2. Check one: Human _____ Zombie _____

3. List work experience. If you are a zombie, and your previous experience was as a mindless servant to an evil sorcerer, please give sorcerer's full name and type of magic practiced.

4. Personal references: List names and telephone numbers of three friends or family members. If you are a zombie, do *not* list your victims. They can no longer be reached by phone. And even if they could, they would not say good things about you.

5. What hours are you available to work? If you are a zombie, do *not* answer "Breakfast, lunch, and dinner, so I can feast on the flesh of slow-moving shoppers."

Chapter 4

Werewolves

A big problem with werewolves is that 27 days out of the month, they are perfectly normal people. But on that 28th day, watch out! The full moon brings on a bad hair day like you would not believe.

Some werewolves don't even realize what they are. They live regular lives during the whole month, then when the full moon pops up, they turn into their monstrous selves. By the next morning, they are back to human form. They might not even remember what happened to them.

They are usually confused about how their clothes got ripped. They often wonder why they spend the next few days pulling bits of rabbit fur out of their teeth. Sadly, many werewolves are so dim, they never figure out the mystery.

> **IMPORTANT SAFETY TIP:** You do not have to be smart to be a werewolf.

It is important to remember that you will turn into a foul creature of the night if a werewolf bites you. The bite does not even have to happen while the other person is in his wolfy form. If you innocently stick your fingers into another person's mouth and he bites down, you could end up howling at the moon.

> **IMPORTANT SAFETY TIP:** Do not become a dentist.

Recognizing werewolves
As already mentioned, werewolves cannot be told apart from normal humans most of the time. But on full moon nights, there are some telltale signs:

1. <u>Transforming when the full moon rises:</u> It is a bad sign if a person starts to twitch, scream, and expand into the shape of a massive wolf. In my experience, that hardly ever turns out well.

When you see this happening, you have a few minutes to get away. During the creature's painful transformation from man to beast, it is too busy to notice how tasty you look.

IMPORTANT SAFETY TIP: Do not stand around watching a werewolf transform. Yes, it looks cool, but when he's done, he will be hungry.

ACTIVITY 4.1
Phases of the Moon

<u>Instructions</u>: Since werewolves are at their most dangerous when the moon is full, below is a chart to identify whether it is safe to venture outside or not.

<u>Note:</u> It is *never* safe to venture outside. But if you insist, compare the moon pictures below to the moon in the sky over your house.

	<u>New Moon</u>: If the moon is invisible, you might think it's not full, but it could be a trick. It might be full, but it's hidden by clouds or behind your Aunt Esther. Stay inside, just to be sure.
	<u>Crescent moon:</u> This small sliver of moon is barely visible, so it does not seem to be full. However, it might be a full moon in the middle of an eclipse. Crouch in the bathtub, eat peanut butter out of the jar for dinner, and hope to survive the night.
	<u>Half moon:</u> Only half of the moon is visible, so you should be safe. Of course, maybe you don't see the other half because it's hidden behind another monster, like a vampire. It's too risky; hide in the cellar.
	<u>Full moon:</u> Stay inside! Lock the doors! Bar the windows! Everyone's gonna die!

Recognizing werewolves (continued)

2. <u>Body covered with thick, dark hair:</u> Now, I am not talking about hair like that guy at the public pool. You know the one I mean? He takes off his shirt and it looks like he's wearing another shirt underneath.

That guy has a gross amount of hair, but werewolves are much worse. Picture the Incredible Hulk. Then cover him from head to toe with fur like a German shepherd's. And like the Hulk, tattered remains of his clothes are hanging off of his body. Now you are starting to get a picture of the werewolf.

IMPORTANT SAFETY TIP: Just to be on the safe side, do not put your fingers in the hairy pool guy's mouth.

---

3. <u>Long, sharp teeth and glowing red eyes:</u> These are two things the werewolf has in common with vampires. The teeth are not exactly the same, though. A werewolf's are huge, like something Tyrannosaurus Rex would have been proud of. A vampire's are smaller and needle-sharp, although they are still unnaturally large for a human.

Glowing red eyes help werewolves and vampires see at night. Both monsters can see in the dark much better than you can. This puts you at a disadvantage every time you turn out a light.

> **IMPORTANT SAFETY TIP:** If you sleep (which you should never do), leave your light on.

4. <u>Howling at the full moon:</u> Anyone who does this has something wrong with him. He may or may not be a werewolf, but does it really matter? A group of people howling at the moon might be monsters looking for a meal, or they might be college students on their way home from a wild party. Either way, you want to avoid the area at all costs.

> **IMPORTANT SAFETY TIP:** Stay away from college students.

Avoiding werewolves

Werewolves can be just about anywhere because they usually look and act like regular humans. It is hard to say who to stay away from, which is one reason werewolves are so dangerous.

If you must go places where people are, there are some spots where you will be safer than others. Ignore this list at your own peril!

1. <u>Zoos:</u> These are very dangerous because they are visited by people who like animals. A person who likes animals too much might see a werewolf and want to pet it, instead of running for his life. If you pet a werewolf, the best thing you can expect is that you will get bitten and become one. If that's the best case scenario, you can imagine how awful the other options are.

Plus, actual wolves live at the zoo. People who like wolves might mistake a werewolf for a regular wolf and get too close. You know what happens then.

2. <u>Church:</u> Unlike vampires, werewolves have no problem entering churches. That should alarm you. However, most church activities take place during the day, so you are fairly safe attending a regular service. On full moon nights, do not visit a church for any reason. In fact, on full moon nights, lock yourself in a bank vault and refuse to open the steel door until morning.

IMPORTANT SAFETY TIP: Store plenty of food, blankets, and reading materials at your bank. If they're willing to guard your money, they should be willing to hang onto a couple pillows and some granola bars for you.

3. <u>Your grandmother's house:</u> *Never* under any conditions visit your grandmother. Have you heard the story of Little Red Riding Hood? This goofball little girl skips off through the woods to bring her grandmother some lunch. By the time she gets to Grandma's, the old lady has been eaten and a monster has taken her place. Then—and this is my favorite part—Red does not even *notice* that her grandmother has turned into a hungry beast. This girl's problems go way beyond simply being attacked by a wolf.

The story tells us that Granny was devoured by a regular wolf, but that's simply not true. It was a werewolf, without a doubt. A normal wolf could never have put on Grandmother's nightgown and talked to Red. It would even be difficult for a werewolf to do those things, but he could manage if he were hungry enough. It must have been embarrassing for him to put on a nightie, though.

For years, regular wolves have been mad about taking the blame for Red's personal problems. I hope this sets the record straight.

IMPORTANT SAFETY TIP: If you carry a basket of food and wear a ridiculous hood, you are asking for trouble.

ACTIVITY 4.2
Woodland Hazards

<u>Instructions:</u> The following creatures can all be found in the forest. Identify which is the most dangerous.

A. A normal wolf

B. A slobbering werewolf

C. A kindly old lady baking cookies in a cabin

D. A basket-wielding little girl in a red hooded cape

Answer: They're all dangerous and exceedingly annoying, but that little girl is the worst. The scent of food coming from her basket attracts not only wolves, werewolves, and hungry old ladies, but also zombies and the scary carnies who work at carnivals.

Avoiding werewolves (continued)

4. <u>The movie theater:</u> This is one of the most dangerous places you can go when trying to avoid werewolves. In the dark theater, you have no way of seeing them transform from their normal human bodies into hairy werewolf ones. By the time the lights go on at the end of the show, you could be surrounded by a roomful of werewolves. They have finished their massive tubs of popcorn and want dessert. You look like dessert.

> **IMPORTANT SAFETY TIP:** Do not allow yourself to be mistaken for Milk Duds or Sno Caps.

5. <u>Water parks:</u> These are usually safe. Like many members of the dog family, werewolves hate taking baths. They dislike pools because they are like giant bathtubs.

Repelling werewolves

1. <u>Act like a jerk all the time:</u> Because werewolves are just normal people most of the time, you can repel them in the same ways you can repel anybody. They will stay away from you if you smell bad or are rude or have an irritating laugh that sounds like a sick donkey. By behaving this way, you will be safe from werewolves. You will also be an out-

cast.

It will doubtless surprise you to learn that I, Tweedy Britches, am an outcast. I made the right choice for my own safety because I am not constantly bothered by hungry werewolves. Of course, it might be nice to hear my phone ring sometimes and know it's not just a wrong number.

My life as an outcast began when I became known for pushing innocent bystanders into monsters so I would have a better chance of escaping. No one gives me credit for the times when I saved people's lives. Like when I helped a busload of elderly nuns who were surrounded by vampires. I had helpfully yelled to them, "Run for your lives, sisters! They just want your bus!" Then I dashed away, screaming in terror. It's true that no good deed goes unpunished.

2. <u>Act like a jerk sometimes:</u> If the lonely life is not for you, then you could try to behave like a civilized person all month, then be unpleasant on full moon nights only. Your friends and family will soon learn to avoid you on those days. Of course, it is always possible that they will get angry with you for treating them badly on the full moon. If that happens, they might not speak to you for the rest of the month. Then you are back to being an outcast full-time.

It is also possible that other people will suspect *you* of

being a werewolf if you are nasty and smelly only when the moon is full. You could be at grave risk of being killed by your friends or relatives if they think you are a werewolf.

> **IMPORTANT SAFETY TIP:** One benefit of being an outcast is that you have no friends or family to try and kill you.

ACTIVITY 4.3
Outcast Benefits

<u>Instructions:</u> Do you suspect that you're an outcast? Congratulations! It could save your life! Add up the advantages that you get to enjoy as what I like to call "a friendless wonder."

1. Not becoming a werewolf
2. No wasted money on soap or deodorant
3. No wasted time attending other people's birthday parties
4. Mailbox not cluttered with holiday cards every December
5. Keeping up with your favorite TV shows because you never have other plans
6. Did I mention not becoming a werewolf?

Caught by a werewolf

If you were unable to avoid werewolves and you find yourself in the clutches of one, Rule Number One is do not panic. They are far more afraid of you than you are of them. No, wait, that's wrong. I'm thinking of snakes.

> **IMPORTANT SAFETY TIP:** Werewolves are not snakes.

Werewolves are not afraid of you at all, but any person with a brain in his head would be terrified of them. Maybe panicking is not such a bad idea. Then, when you are done panicking, you can try these tactics to save yourself.

1. <u>Try to escape:</u> This is the same as your first line of defense when you run into a vampire or a zombie. Keep in mind that werewolves are fast. They can easily outrun a human, whether he is on foot or on his bike.

> **IMPORTANT SAFETY TIP:** Never ride your bike.

If you are not old enough to drive a car, you could jump on a bus to escape from a werewolf. Unfortunately, we know all about how vampires love riding the bus. Going from a street teeming with werewolves to a bus full of vampires is not an improvement. It is an example of that old saying, "Jumping from the frying pan into the fire."

> **IMPORTANT SAFETY TIP:** Avoid the frying pan, the fire, *and* the bus.

If you can distract the werewolf, you might have time to get away. Remember that werewolves are related to dogs, so you can throw a bone and see if he chases it. If you do not have a bone, try throwing a Frisbee.

Some werewolves are champion Frisbee catchers. Unfortunately, once the werewolf catches the Frisbee, he will carry it right back to you. If you did not escape quickly enough, you will be stuck with a Frisbee that is covered in monster drool. You will also be looking at a werewolf who has worked up an appetite playing Frisbee.

I once heard about a lady who took the werewolves' connection to dogs to a new level. She smacked an attacking werewolf on the nose with a rolled-up newspaper while saying, "Bad dog!" The werewolf ate her and devoured the newspaper, too.

IMPORTANT SAFETY TIP: Werewolves eat newspaper because it adds fiber to their meaty diets. Do not be a paper delivery person.

ACTIVITY 4.4
Werewolf Escape Quiz

<u>Instructions:</u> Identify which of the following is the best way to escape from a werewolf.

    A. Run away.
    B. Pedal away on your bike.
    C. Jump on the bus.
    D. Toss a Frisbee off the edge of a pier.

<u>Answer:</u> *You are correct if you said none of the above. The best way to escape from a werewolf is to trap it in a sturdy sack.*
No, wait, that's snakes again.

Caught by a werewolf (continued)

2. <u>Kill the werewolf:</u> If you cannot escape from the hungry monster, then you have no choice but to kill it. The best way to kill a werewolf is to have your pet mongoose attack it. Werewolves and mongooses hate each other. No, wait, that's snakes again. A mongoose will fight a hissing cobra, but it is smart enough to flee from a werewolf.

> **IMPORTANT SAFETY TIP:** Do not waste your money on a mongoose.

Anyway, back to killing werewolves. First, you need to get your hands on a bullet made of silver. Then find an adult with a gun, like a police officer, and ask him to shoot the werewolf using your bullet. This is not easy to do. Police are trained to avoid firing their guns whenever possible. They are certainly not going to shoot someone just because you say that person turns into a werewolf once a month.

Even if the creature is in its wolfy form, the police officer will probably think it is a person wearing a costume. The officer will use that as an excuse to not shoot the werewolf. In addition to being trained to avoid firing their guns at flesh-eating monsters, police are also trained to not believe in werewolves.

> **IMPORTANT SAFETY TIP:** Police training needs to be improved.

Not only is it hard to find someone to shoot a werewolf for you, but simply getting your hands on a silver bullet is nearly impossible. They are not sold in stores, and even if they were, the bullets would be expensive because they are made of a rare metal.

You could melt down your mother's silverware to make a bullet, but most of the stuff that is called silverware is not actually made of silver. It is stainless steel, and it can barely slice a green bean, let alone kill a werewolf. Even if your mother does have real silver knives and forks, you should not try to turn them into silver bullets. If she finds out, you will have bigger problems than just a werewolf.

> **IMPORTANT SAFETY TIP:** Mothers are protective of their silverware.

ACTIVITY 4.5
Silver Items

<u>Instructions:</u> Identify which of the following items you can melt down to make a silver bullet.

- A. Silver jewelry
- B. Silverware
- C. Second-place Olympic medals
- D. Your brother's coin collection

<u>Answer:</u> *You are correct if you chose none of the above. Your mother will not let you play with fire to melt any of these items. For goodness sake, she doesn't even let you make microwave popcorn by yourself.*

Caught by a werewolf (continued)

Unfortunately, even if you manage to find a silver bullet somehow, there is not much you can do with it. The police are not going to shoot the monster, and you have little hope of driving the bullet barehanded into a werewolf. Like vampires, werewolves tend to fight back when they know you are trying to kill them.

While the best way to kill a werewolf is to shoot it with a silver bullet, there are other ways to get rid of one. For instance, you could cut off its head. Cutting off a monster's head will kill pretty much any kind of creature, except a hydra. A hydra is a monster from Greek mythology that was a multi-headed, snakelike thing. It would grow two heads to replace every one that was cut off. Killing a hydra was really tricky—but that is a subject for another book.

IMPORTANT SAFETY TIP: A book about killing hydras might come in handy, but don't risk going outside to buy it.

Becoming a werewolf

If you could not avoid werewolves and failed to escape

from them or kill them, then you will probably be bitten by one. The bite will transform you into a werewolf at the next full moon. But don't worry. This is not the end of the world.

You can lead a perfectly normal life for almost every night of the month. Then when the full moon rises, you turn into a wild, hairy beast with a taste for human flesh. It is not what most people would choose, but it could be worse. For example, if you were a zombie, you would be brainless and undead all month long.

> **IMPORTANT SAFETY TIP:** There is never a good time to be a zombie.

If you become a werewolf, try to make your plans around the moon. You can buy a calendar that tells you when the moon will be full. Do not allow yourself to be around groups of people on those nights. You might have to come up with excuses for why you cannot attend family events, like your grandmother's birthday party. But you are not supposed to visit your grandmother anyway, remember? Problem solved.

Of course, now that you are already a werewolf, I suppose you can start visiting your grandma again. Just do not go when there is a full moon. The last thing that poor woman needs is for her grandchild to transform into a werewolf, eat her, then dress in her nightgown to lure others into a hungry belly. Show Granny some respect. That woman changed your poopy diapers when you were a baby.

> **IMPORTANT SAFETY TIP:** Resist the urge to wear your grandmother's clothes.

I'd like to make one final comment. This werewolf chapter has special meaning for me. Remember that story at the beginning of this book about the trick-or-treater who spent Halloween night in a hole, being subjected to a shower of monster drool? That chocolate-loving kid in the Superman costume was me. Werewolves were the first monsters I ever encountered, and if it hadn't been for a convenient grave that someone had left lying around, I wouldn't be here today. Because of that first experience, I feel a bond with people who are defending themselves against werewolves. And I can't look at a pair of blue tights without breaking into a cold sweat.

Tweedy Britches

Chapter 5
Witches

All the monsters mentioned so far—vampires, zombies, and werewolves—are interested in turning you into lunch. Or they want to turn you into a monster just like them. Or both. Witches are different. They don't want to eat you or turn you into a witch. No, these evil women attack humans for different reasons:

1. They might want a human servant to work for them, so they're trying to enslave someone.

2. They might want to try out some new spells and need a guinea pig.

3. They might simply be in a bad mood and want to mess with somebody.

Regardless of why the witch is interested in you, it's important to understand how to keep yourself safe from becoming a witch's newest unwilling housekeeper, experiment, or toy.

> **IMPORTANT SAFETY TIP:** If a witch uses you as a guinea pig, you might *literally* be turned into a guinea pig.

Recognizing witches

When you read the word "witch," many of you probably imagine the type of witches that are found in books about wizarding schools. You get a picture in your mind of a cute girl wearing an English school uniform, waving a wand and giggling. That is not the sort of witch we're talking about here.

The evil witches that are a threat to you are not pleasant, normal people who happen to have some magical powers. If you believe that you can sit next to a witch in class and share a glass of pumpkin juice with her in the dining hall, then you are as nutty as the witch who lost control of her broomstick and landed in a pecan tree.

> **IMPORTANT SAFETY TIP:** Stay out from under pecan trees.

Do not be fooled by authors and moviemakers who mislead you about the true nature of witches. Chances are, these people are witches themselves, or are acting under a witch's spell.

The truth is that evil witches are mean-spirited women who cast cruel spells. There are no male witches of the evil, spell-casting variety. Some witches are more bad-tempered than others, but none of them like humans. Perhaps more importantly, none of them *are* humans.

Also, do not confuse evil witches with women who believe in maintaining a strong connection with animals and nature. These are normal humans who might call themselves witches, but they don't cast nasty spells or force humans into serving them.

For one thing, some "normal" human witches connect to nature by running around the woods under a full moon with no clothes on. I'm not saying this is a good idea—refer to the werewolf chapter regarding full moons—but it's not a risk to public health. Evil witches on the other hand are hideous, and they *always* wear clothes—lots of clothes. Evil witches do this as a public service; they might be cruel, but no one is that cruel.

> **IMPORTANT SAFETY TIP:** You do *not* want to see an evil witch naked.

There are a few telltale signs that help you identify scary, dangerous, evil witches. Sometimes they try to disguise themselves, but you will never be fooled if you know what to look for.

1. <u>Warts</u>: All witches have them—lots of them. The ones you'll notice are on their faces. Believe me, though, they also have warts in other unpleasant spots. For instance, under no circumstances should you ever look at the bottoms of a witch's feet. And take seriously the **IMPORTANT SAFETY TIP** above about not seeing a witch naked.

The older and more evil a witch is, the more warts she will have. They will spring up on her nose and chin first, then sprout long, curly, black hairs. Many people who see witches wonder why they don't remove these hideous warts. After all, can't a witch use her magic to at least make the hairs stop growing?

There are different theories about this. Some think that a witch's source of power is in her warts. That is why the oldest and most powerful have the most and biggest warts. Others think that having big, nasty warts is like wearing a badge of honor for witches.

It's kind of like when a boxer wins an important fight and they give him that big, ridiculous-looking metal belt as a prize. They are pretty much saying that only the meanest, toughest person can get away with wearing such an ugly belt because no one in his right mind would dare make fun of him. In the case of witches, only the oldest, most powerful can be covered with warts and not have to worry about people mocking them.

> **IMPORTANT SAFETY TIP:** Just because a person—like your school bus driver, for instance—has a big, hairy wart on her nose, that does not always mean she is a witch. But she probably is.

2. <u>Might be Green:</u> Not all witches are green. People think they are because the Wicked Witch of the West was. What most people do not understand is that witches are only green if they don't wash. If they do not wash, they end up covered in moss, just like a tree or that weird boy down the block who was never quite right after falling off the monkey bars.

Some witches refuse to wash just because they are lazy, but others are actually allergic to water. This was why the Wicked Witch of the West melted when that annoying kid from Kansas dumped a bucket on her.

> **IMPORTANT SAFETY TIP:** Melted witch feet are impossible to clean out of your ruby slippers.

3. <u>Silly Hats:</u> Witches always wear hats, and they aren't normal hats, either. No baseball caps or knit ski hats for these folks. Witches often wear tall, pointy, traditional witchy-style hats with wide brims.

No one knows why anyone would bother with such impractical headwear. They are too tall, so witches must duck through doorways. They are too wide, so they catch the breeze and blow off. And they are not meant to keep a person's ears warm in the winter. They are not stylish, either, because they look like giant, upside-down black snow cones cups.

Some witches realize that the upside-down snow cone look is ridiculous, and they choose hats that are even uglier. Usually the hats themselves are small and made of ratty old velvet. They are covered with folds of netting and hunks of fake fruit that dangle around the witch's face.

Some creative witches practice taxidermy, which is a hobby that involves preserving and stuffing the dead bodies of birds and small animals. The witches glue these unfortunate deceased creatures to their hats. The result makes witches look like they are being swarmed by angry wildlife.

IMPORTANT SAFETY TIP: Avoid anyone with dead squirrels and possums hovering around her ears.

4. Clothes: One advantage of being a witch is the comfortable wardrobe. Witches never spend time working out at the gym, so they are flabby. In order to hide the flab, they wear long, loose dresses and shapeless cloaks with hoods.

Their clothes are usually black or gray or dark brown. Most witches believe dark colors help them blend into the night so they can more easily surprise their victims. This means that most people never see the large, warty woman in a baggy dress who jumps out of the dark and turns them into a slug. Lucky them.

5. A familiar: Many witches have animal companions that add to the witches' power. These are called familiars. Common familiars are black cats or toads. There are many witches, however, who dare to be different. For instance, some keep dogs instead of cats as familiars. This doesn't make much sense.

The primary job of a familiar is to be a lookout when the witch is up to evil deeds. Familiars also help catch gross insects for the witch's potions. Dogs are not much good for either of these tasks. While cats and toads are good lookouts because they are small, quiet, and can see in the dark, dogs are large, loud, and smell bad when they are left outdoors in rainy weather.

> **IMPORTANT SAFETY TIP:** Witches also stink when they get wet.

Dogs make especially poor lookouts because they start barking whenever anybody drives by. Sometimes they abandon their posts when they decide to chase a car or the mailman or a tennis ball thrown by the witch's enemy. You would never catch a cat retrieving a ball thrown by anyone.

A dog familiar also can't help a witch catch bugs or rodents for her potions because dogs have big mouths and tend to accidentally swallow anything they catch. If a witch sends her dog out to catch three dragonflies, two tadpoles, and one salamander, the dog will come home hours later with nothing but a stomachache.

On the upside, sometimes the dog might come home carrying a whole salami in his mouth because he didn't know the difference between salami and salamander and was embarrassed to ask. A little dog slobber doesn't bother witches, so they pull out the rye bread and mustard for a salami feast.

There are some witches that choose other unusual familiars, like ferrets and ravens. These animals can turn out surprisingly well because they are small and move silently in the dark. Other animals, like rhinos, aren't a great choice. Because of their huge size, overpowering odor, and complete refusal to follow orders, rhinos make poor familiars.

> **IMPORTANT SAFETY TIP:** Rhinos also make rotten pets, lousy bus drivers, and uncooperative dairy cows.

Avoiding Witches

The best way to keep from being attacked by a witch is to steer clear of places where witches like to hang out. This is easy for most people, since witches spend most of their time in smelly, dirty spots like abandoned dungeons and high school chemistry labs. However, there are a few spots where witches can turn up unexpectedly. Always be on guard.

1. <u>Your backyard under a full moon at midnight:</u> How many times has this happened to you? You are sleeping soundly, when you wake up wanting a drink of water. You go downstairs to the kitchen and peek out the window over the sink as you're filling your glass. In the backyard you see a circle of witches dancing and performing spells under the moonlight. Their big, loose dresses are billowing in the breeze, and starlight reflects off their huge warts and impractical hats.

You have probably wondered what to do when this occurs. Should you go out there and order the witches off your property before their rhinos trample your mom's flowerbeds? Or is it better to creep back to bed and pull the covers over your head?

Let me assure you that the most important thing is to stay out of your yard. There are witches out there, for crying out loud! Remember that you're supposed to avoid witches! Leave them alone, go back to your room, and if it will make you feel better, sleep in the closet with the door closed and the light on. Actually, that's not a bad idea whether there are witches in your backyard or not. Yes, the flowers might get trampled, but better them than you, right?

ACTIVITY 5.1
Fun with Witches

<u>Instructions:</u> If you want to see what will happen to someone who disturbs the witches in your yard, but wisely do not want to take risks with your own personal safety, try the following.

Step 1: Call your most irritating neighbor. You know, the one who won't give back your golf balls when you shoot them into his swimming pool? Your neighbor will be asleep because it's the middle of the night, so he will be groggy and annoyed that you are calling. That's fun all by itself.

Step 2: Quickly explain to him that you just saw a bunch of kids swimming in his pool. When they were done, they ran into your yard, where your dog cornered them. Tell your neighbor that he should come over quickly to help you deal with the kids. Remember to talk fast so he does not fall back to sleep while you are on the phone.

Step 3: Watch out your window as your neighbor runs out of his backdoor and into your yard where the witches are.

Fun with Witches Activity (continued)

He will probably carry a useless weapon over his shoulder to scare the kids, like a shovel or a garden gnome statue.

Step 4: The next morning, explain to your parents that you do not know where Mr. Johnson is. You also have no idea who owns the dented shovel and torn bathrobe in your backyard. And as far as you know, that patch of scorched grass has always been there.

Step 5: Repeat with another irritating neighbor. This activity is especially entertaining for sleepovers with your friends.

Avoiding witches (continued)

2. <u>The Gym:</u> If you are serious about avoiding witches, the gym is a safe place to go. Remember that witches wear baggy, dark clothes that hide their flabby, out-of-shape bodies. This means that they are not going to waste time on a treadmill or lifting weights.

In addition to a general dislike of exercise, some witches are allergic to water, so they avoid pools. Of course, they all refuse to shave their legs and look horrible in bathing suits, so it is a good thing that they do not often swim.

3. <u>The veterinarian's office:</u> Since most witches have animal familiars, they have to keep the animals healthy. That's not an easy task because familiars have access to a lot of unusual items in their witch owners' cupboards. Things like pickled bat's wings and the legs of dragonflies are as common in witches' kitchens as peanut butter and wilted lettuce are in yours. The witches' familiars often get into the gross items in the cabinets, and they snarf them down. Then the animal gets a tummy ache and needs to visit the veterinarian.

Having familiars as patients isn't much fun for the vets or everyone in the vet's waiting room. Imagine the shock of a German shepherd that innocently wants to sniff a cat it sees resting on its owner's flabby lap. The next thing the dog knows, there's a puff of green smoke, and he has been turned into a turnip. No, this is not any fun for the dog, and it is even worse for every pet owner in the waiting room. They are now being terrorized by a wild-eyed witch with a still-smoking wand in her hand.

For every cute, fuzzy puppy a veterinarian sees, there are at least three witches' toads that have swallowed too much powdered harpy blood. And you do *not* want to know how the poor vet gets it out. Just a hint: It involves vinegar, rubber gloves, and a long straw.

> **IMPORTANT SAFETY TIP:** Do not become a vet.

4. <u>Dark, Creepy Castle:</u> Here's the thing about dark, creepy castles: All sorts of scary monsters hang around them. Witches, vampires, zombies, wolfmen, you name it. Dark, creepy castles are like coffee houses for monsters. They sit on dusty furniture, pick spiders out of cups of whatever disgusting beverages they're drinking, and talk about what they would do to any unfortunate humans who might show up at the castle. Do *you* want to be that unfortunate human? I didn't think so.

> **IMPORTANT SAFETY TIP:** Creepy castles are always dusty because the housekeepers keep getting eaten.

ACTIVITY 5.2
Creepy Castle Pop Quiz

<u>Instructions:</u> Answer the following question using your newfound knowledge about monsters.

Your family is driving down a dark, deserted road, and the car breaks down. You remember that you passed a creepy castle a little way back. You wonder if someone should walk back there to call a tow truck. Which of the following should you do?

A. Leave your family in the car while you walk back to the castle by yourself. When an unusually hairy guy answers the door and howls at you, explain about your car trouble. Point out that you are a weak, tasty human and have no way to escape the woods on your own. He will know exactly what to do.

B. Stay safely in the car with the rest of your family while you send your older brother back to the castle. Make sure he tells the castle owner that his whole family is helpless and alone in a disabled car nearby.

Creepy Castle Pop Quiz Activity (continued)

C. Get everyone out of the car, grab your sleeping bags from the trunk, and carry them back to the castle. Explain to the pale guy who answers the door that it is dark and spooky outside, and you would like to spend a cozy, warm night in his guest room.

D. Are you kidding? If you even think about visiting this castle, then you have not learned a thing so far in this book. Go back to page 1 and start over.

Answer: The correct answer to this question depends on what your plans are for the future. If you would like to have a future as a living human, then definitely go with answer D and avoid that castle. On the other hand, if you prefer to become a werewolf, or have your blood drained by a vampire, or be eaten by a zombie, then you should choose answer A, B, or C. Any of them will do.

Avoiding witches (continued)

5. <u>Dentist's Office:</u> Dentists and their patients are usually safe from witches. Since no one is likely to kiss witches, the hags figure there is no point in brushing their teeth. And since they do not hang around with anyone besides other monsters, keeping a shiny white smile is not at the top of a witch's to-do list. On top of that, witches prefer to be the ones causing the pain, instead of having someone else inflict it on them.

For all of these reasons, witches rarely visit the dentist. Becoming a dentist is a good career move if you are afraid of witches. As discussed earlier, however, it increases the risk of werewolf bites.

IMPORTANT SAFETY TIP: All jobs are risky. Let your parents support you forever.

ACTIVITY 5.3
Witch Identification Test

Instructions: Since witches do not visit the dentist, they have more rotten, falling-out teeth than most people. If you think your sister or mom or school bus driver might be a witch, there is a simple test to see if you are correct.

Step 1: Reach into her mouth and poke around to see if any of her teeth are loose or missing. If they are, then this person is actually a horrible, evil witch who has disguised herself as a human (or a school bus driver).

Step 2: Yank your hand out of the witch's mouth and run. The only thing more dangerous than a normal witch is an angry witch whose sore, rotten teeth have just been prodded by some nosy kid.

Step 3: If the person's teeth all feel solid and seem to be in the right spots, you should still run. The only thing more dangerous than an angry witch is your mom or sister or bus driver after you've stuck your grimy fingers in her mouth.

> **IMPORTANT SAFETY TIP:** Never try this hand-in-the-mouth activity on someone who might be a werewolf or vampire.
>
> **EXTRA IMPORTANT SAFETY TIP:** Although walking is good exercise, do not try this experiment on your bus driver if it is winter and you live more than one mile from school.

Repelling Witches

Witches are afraid of humans, so if you see one, she will probably stand really still and hope you don't see her. No, wait, that's rabbits. Witches are not rabbits. If you see a witch, she will probably attack you, instead of running away from you. Maybe if *you* stay very still, the witch will not see you and she will go away. Or maybe not. Instead there is a chance she will mistake you for a rabbit and put you in her stew.

> **IMPORTANT SAFETY TIP:** Witches like stew.

ACTIVITY 5.4
Learning from Rabbits

<u>Instructions:</u> Rabbits have many clever ways to escape from creatures that want to eat them. Some of these strategies could work for you, too. Next time a witch is chasing you, select one of the following to help you avoid capture.

A. Freeze in place like a statue.
B. Use your strong back legs to hop away.
C. Dig a network of holes in your yard where you can hide from danger.
D. Say you're the Easter Bunny and offer her jelly beans if she doesn't cast a spell on you.

Repelling witches (continued)

All right, so you have accidentally run into a witch and you need to figure out how to keep the hag from chasing you. This is tricky, but there are a few tactics that have worked for me in the past.

1. <u>Separate them:</u> Witches usually live in groups called covens. They live with other witches for a number of reasons. For one thing, this allows them to protect one another from gangs of angry humans who are tired of being attacked by witches. Being around other witches also gives them the opportunity to teach each other spells and share potion recipes.

Most important, living in covens gives the witches some company when they are sitting around watching TV at night. Enjoying celebrity dancing shows together is a great way to wind down after a hard day of terrorizing school children and turning police officers into yaks.

IMPORTANT SAFETY TIP: Don't be a police officer or a school child.

You can keep witches away by forcing them to separate from the rest of their coven before they can get close to you. In many ways, witches are like cows because they resist being separated from the rest of their herd.

> **IMPORTANT SAFETY TIP:** Some witches have also been spotted chewing their cud.

If you see a witch and are afraid that she might follow you, try ducking into a voting booth. You are pretty safe at a polling place because people must enter the voting booth one at a time. The witch will avoid this since she is not allowed to bring the rest of her coven in with her. She will forget about you, rather than leaving the other witches outside.

Other places that witches avoid because they don't want to be separated from one another include public bathroom stalls, clothing store dressing rooms, and the written driving test area at the Department of Motor Vehicles. If you can figure out a way to stay in spots where people must be alone, then witches will not go there and you will be safe. Unfortunately, these places tend not to be much fun. You must decide if you would rather spend your life in a public bathroom stall or risk running into witches.

> **IMPORTANT SAFETY TIP:** Living in the bus station bathroom might not be bad if you spruce it up with some new paint and a massive air freshener.

2. <u>Things that smell good:</u> Witches hate sweet, flowery scents, and they especially do not want to smell that way. Carry a bottle of perfume with you to spritz on any witches that might be attracted to you. Better yet, never leave home without one of those women from the department store who tries to spray customers with perfume. You would be totally safe from witches with one of those women around you. Of course, your friends and family would probably avoid you, too.

> **IMPORTANT SAFETY TIP:** You are always safe from witches at the mall perfume counter, but remember that the mall is full of vampires.

To be on the safe side, you might want to bathe in a vat of perfume every morning. Sure, you will reek and the only people who will be near you have severely clogged noses. You will have the last laugh, though, when everyone else is attacked by a witch while you are perfectly safe.

Caught by a Witch

No matter how hard you try to avoid witches, someday you might still find yourself surrounded by an angry coven of hags. Some of them are trying to get a piece of you for their potions, while others are experimenting with a new spell that turns humans into dining room chairs or pumpkin seeds or something. No matter what the witches want, you need to escape. When trapped by witches, try one of the following:

1. <u>Throw water at them.</u> As mentioned earlier, not all witches are allergic to water, but some are. If you're surrounded by say, ten witches, figure that at least two can't stand water. The number is higher if they have green skin. If you toss a water balloon at each one, hopefully some will melt.

There are a couple of problems with this strategy, however. First, you have to carry around a lot of water at all times so you can hurl it at witches when necessary. Most people refuse to always drag around a fire hose.

IMPORTANT SAFETY TIP: Those people will be attacked by witches.

Another problem with this strategy is that the rest of the witches you douse with water will not be allergic to it. Instead of melting, these witches will just be wet, and witches enjoy being wet as much as your cat does. The only difference is that your cat cannot cast a spell that will turn you into a fire hydrant in the middle of a dog show.

2. Set them on fire: Like vampires, witches burn. But also like vampires, they don't want to. The old fashioned method for burning witches was to tie them to a wooden pole, then pile branches and leaves around their feet, and set the brush on fire. Sounds easy, right? Wrong!

If you have been paying attention, you already know that witches are dangerous because they cast spells against people they don't like. And if you are tying them to a tree and tucking dried twigs around them, you have suddenly shot up to the top of their "People I Don't Like" list. In other words, while you are trying to set the witch on fire, she is busy turning your eyebrows into pickles and making you smell like rotten cheese. No one wins.

Be aware that only the witch who casts a curse can reverse it. If you set this witch on fire before she reverses the spell, you are in for a lonely life, Pickle Brow.

> **IMPORTANT SAFETY TIP:** A burning witch will not reverse her spell.

3. <u>Drown them:</u> A long time ago, people believed that witches were unable to swim. They believed that witches were afraid of deep water like lakes, pools, and large bowls of soup. Unfortunately, it is not true that witches can't swim. Sure, some can't, just like some humans can't. And some are allergic to water. But many can swim, and they just get annoyed at someone who pushes them into a lake or attacks them with a can of chicken noodle.

The rumor about witches not swimming started many years ago when few people—neither humans or witches—could swim. There were no YMCA's to give swim lessons back then.

Back then, bathing suits were huge, heavy woolen outfits that reached from people's necks to their ankles. These suits got so heavy when they were wet that they often dragged their owners to the bottom of the lake. Even Olympic swimmers frequently drowned in shallow water because of their 100-pound sopping wet bathing suits. So it was just a coincidence that witches tended to drown. Everyone else drowned, too.

Today, bathing suits are a lot smaller and they are lighter when they get soaked. Still, some witches never learn to swim simply because, let's face it, they don't exactly look their best in a teeny bikini. On the other hand, some witches are so mean that they learn to swim just so they will have an excuse to make others see them in a skimpy bathing suit.

ACTIVITY 5.5
Beach-Going Witches

Instructions: Pick out the items that are needed when a witch goes to the beach.

1. A bathing suit
2. A swim cap
3. Nose plug
4. Flippers
5. A blindfold

Answer: *All of the above are important. Items 1-4 are for the witch. The blindfold is for anyone else at the beach who has to see her in a swimsuit.*

Caught by a witch (continued)

4. <u>Take her wand:</u> Witches carry wands that they use to focus their magic for spells. These are simply sticks of wood that came from magical hissing trees in the Ancient Murdering Forest of Blood. Anybody can get one, as long as they're willing to brave the mutant crab ants, electrified grass, and flying sharks.

> **IMPORTANT SAFETY TIP:** The Ancient Murdering Forest of Blood is even less fun than it sounds.

A witch loses a great deal of her power if she doesn't have her wand, so this is a good way to weaken the witch so you can escape. Because they are so important, wands are usually kept hidden except when they are actually being used to cast a spell. That's why you can't always identify a witch by her wand.

However, sometimes you know for sure that someone is a witch. Like if she and her familiar have cornered you in a haunted house and she has already turned your hair into electric eels. In this case, you can try to steal her wand and use it to escape. There is only one small problem with this plan: The witch will put up a serious fight to maintain control of her wand.

If you are the captain of your school's wrestling team, that training will come in handy when trying to take a witch's wand away. If you cannot overpower the witch by being a wrestler, or a defensive tackle for the Chicago Bears, or Ironman, then your best bet is to distract her while you steal the wand.

An example of a good distraction is to yell, "Hey, is your rhino supposed to be eating all that dried harpy blood?" While she checks to see if the animal needs to visit the vet, you can rip the wand out of her hand and make a break for it. If the wand is not in her hand, you will have to stick your hand into her pocket to get it. Unfortunately for you, witches keep all sorts of nasty, squishy things in their pockets.

IMPORTANT SAFETY TIP: Next time you are at the doctor's office, swipe some of those rubber gloves. They'll come in handy during your next witch encounter.

Once you have the wand, you could try to use it against her. Try pointing it at the witch and making up some nonsense that sounds like a spell. (For example: "Chocolate spider, ice cream bee. Get this hag away from me!") Probably nothing will happen, but you might get lucky and blow off some of the witch's warts. While she's busy trying to reattach them, you can run away.

Sadly, a witch's wand rarely works for anyone but the witch herself. Plus, you are a human with no magical power. Your best bet is to just break the wand so it can't be used against you, then hurl the pieces at the witch while you escape. They might poke her in the eye and slow her down.

Becoming a Witch

Witches are not like vampires or werewolves or zombies because a person does not become one simply by being bitten. Witches are born, not made. This is both good news and bad news for you.

On the plus side, if you are caught by a witch and cannot escape by fire or water, then you do not have to worry about being turned into a witch. There is no spell or curse or bite that will transform you into an evil, ugly hag.

On the downside, if you are caught by a witch, it usually means she has some really unpleasant plans for you. The witch might have caught a human because she needs someone to practice new spells on. Possibly she needs a human assistant, so she will use a mind control curse so you will do anything she says. Don't even bother trying to explain that to the police. When you are caught robbing a bank, saying "My witch master made me do it," is not going to fly.

Another alternative is that the witch who catches you might need a nanny for her baby witch. This is very bad. The only thing more annoying than a full-grown witch is a baby one. They have lots of magical power but no control over it. Spells fly around the nursery, bouncing off walls, bursting through windows, and wiggling through keyholes to cause trouble throughout the whole house. Try feeding apple sauce to a kid who can make a whole apple tree sprout out of the spoon. Naps are more dangerous than a stampede of rabid buffalo. Few witch nannies have ever survived bath time.

> **IMPORTANT SAFETY TIP:** Never take your eyes off the rubber duckie.

In the long run, maybe you would be better off if witches could turn you into one of their own kind. Or maybe you should hope that you are caught by a vampire or a zombie instead. At least they won't make you babysit.

IMPORTANT SAFETY TIP: The worse part of babysitting for a witch: *No tips!*

Conclusion

There you have it. You have just read a complete guide to keeping yourself safe from monsters that want to eat you, attack you, and/or transform you into a dreadful creature of evil. With all this information at your fingertips, you should be able to protect yourself under any conditions. Unless of course you run into a different kind of monster, like a mummy, a ghost, or Bigfoot. Those creatures pose whole new sets of problems, and they are a subject for another book.

IMPORTANT SAFETY TIP: Do not leave your house to buy that other book. You took your life into your hands going out to buy this one.

Just remember, it's a monster jungle out there. Be careful and good luck!

##

What are you doing for the next few minutes?

I know you're not going anywhere because you just finished reading *This Bites*, which has taught you to avoid leaving the house. So, since you're wisely staying inside to avoid all the monsters that are roaming around outdoors, you've got time on your hands. Please use that time to write a review of this book.

A lot of other readers want to know what you think about it so they can decide whether or not to read it. Reviews on Amazon, Barnes & Noble, Goodreads, etc. are vital to a book's success. Be honest—you check out reviews before deciding what to read, right? Everyone does, which is why reviews are so important to authors and the reading public.

You can help people protect themselves from monster attacks by writing a review. A review says that you read the book, and you haven't been eaten by a monster. It proves that *This Bites* is doing its job.

Of course, I hope you'll say the book is hilarious, exciting, and full of helpful advice that has allowed you to avoid becoming lunch, but whether you choose to say that or not, I'd be grateful if you would please write a review. It doesn't have to be long—just a sentence or two is enough. Although feel free to go into detail. Feel free to tell readers that the book is the most important piece of literature to be published this century. Say the author is charming, intelligent, and—you can tell, even without a photo—devastatingly handsome.

Thanks in advance for taking the time to complete a review. When you're done, please check out the other great titles from my publisher at: www.KissingFrogBooks.com. You'll find Bigfoot, ghosts, and one about a graveyard that kept me up at night. Of course, I'm always up at night. Since taping that zombie face over my bed, I haven't slept a wink.

Happy reading!

Tweedy Britches

What's next from Tweedy Britches?

He's taking a brief break from monsters to help kids with another big, hairy problem—school. His upcoming book is called *THIS WILL BE ON THE TEST: A FIELD GUIDE TO SCHOOL*. If you liked "Important Safety Tips" in *THIS BITES*, you'll love "Fun School Facts" in this new book. Be on the lookout for it at your favorite booksellers. Here's a sample to get you all excited. That's called a "teaser," and although it's cruel, it's kind of fun at the same time.

THIS WILL BE ON THE TEST
A Field Guide to School

When you were little, you probably looked forward to starting school. Your older brothers and sisters went off every morning with their lunch bags, and you couldn't wait to go with them.

When you were finally old enough to go, you woke up extra early and teased your little brother about how he had to stay home like a baby. You felt all grown-up wearing your backpack, standing at the bus stop with the big kids.

It was an exciting day with lots of new people and a nice teacher. There was fun stuff to do, like coloring, singing, and games. There was also not-so-fun stuff, like sitting still with your hands folded, talking with "indoor voices," and walking slowly in single file lines. And what was that nonsense about having to raise your hand before going to the bathroom?

The next morning your mom woke you up for your second day of school. You rolled over and said, "No, thanks, I'm staying home today."

That's when your mom burst out laughing.

"School isn't for just one day!" she exclaimed. "You'll be going every day for the next 13 years. Even more if you go to college."

No! *Every day*? For *how many* years?

On the second morning of school you glared at your little brother, who was perched on the couch, munching a bowl of Cheerios. He was still in his pajamas, watching cartoons.

"You're so lucky you get to go to school," he said. "I can't wait until I can go, too."

You wanted to dump the cereal over his goofy little head.

> **Fun School Fact:**
>
> An *anagram* is when you take the letters of a word or phrase and rearrange them to create a new word or phrase. For instance, "funeral" becomes "real fun." An anagram of "kindergarten" is "dark entering." That gives you a hint at how disturbing school really is.

Since you're stuck going to school, you can probably use a little help getting through it. That's where this book comes in. It unravels the mysteries of school and tries to make these years in captivity a little easier.

Maybe you think that's an awful lot to ask from one book. Okay, how about something more realistic: If you're reading this book in school, your teacher will think you're busy and she won't go looking for more work to give you. As an added bonus, this is more interesting than your math book. Yes, even the label on your sweatshirt is more interesting than your math book, but if your teacher catches you reading your clothing, she'll figure you need the dreaded "something to keep you busy." Avoid that problem by burying your nose in this book where you might learn something useful.

MORE MONSTERS and LAUGHS from KISSING FROG BOOKS

Bigfoot CSI

When a Bigfoot dies in the forest, and no one is there to see, does it still leave a body? Sixteen-year-old Piper O'Connell knows it does, and it's her job to dispose of those bodies before they are discovered by human hunters. Not that she wants the job. It's dangerous, the hours are lousy, and all she'll get at the end of her career—assuming she survives—is a collection of worthless trinkets from the Bigfoot families she helped. When someone connected to Piper and the Bigfoot community is murdered, it's up to her to find the killer before she becomes the next victim.

Full to Bursting

My name is John Regan. I moved to Chicago in seventh grade when my dad got a new job. I expected to be a friendless, pathetic earthworm at my new school, leaving slime trails in the halls for more popular kids to slip on. I didn't expect that my bizarre grandmother would move in, or a creepy kid would stalk my house, or my teacher would be a vampire. But what I really never expected was that it would be a blast.

Graveyard Kids

When a brother and sister discover that there's no date of death on an ancient tombstone in the graveyard by their house, they wonder what happened to the woman whose name is on it. The little brother is convinced she became a vampire, so his sister must find a more rational explanation—otherwise she'll have to admit that vampires are real and her goofy little brother was right about something.

Stones of Abraxas

Book One in the *World of Abraxas Series*

David Stanhope seems like an average twelve-year-old, but there's a secret lurking in his attic that's been sought by an evil sorcerer for hundreds of years. If he discovers that David and his sister Amanda have it, he will destroy them. Maybe David isn't so average after all.

Heroes of Abraxas

Book Two in the *World of Abraxas Series*

When David Stanhope and his sister Amanda unearthed a huge ruby in their family's attic last summer, it launched them on the adventure of a lifetime. Now, a year later, they're back home, trying to lead normal lives. Until a knock at their door propels them into dangerous power struggles in the magical world of Abraxas once again.

About the Author

About the author: Tweedy Britches is in sixth grade at Bram Stoker Middle School in Senoia, Georgia. He might be young, but he has already spent years learning the secrets of avoiding monsters, escaping from monsters, destroying monsters, and helping other people stay safe from monsters. Now he uses his expertise to help keep others from becoming part of a monster menu.

If you want to contact Tweedy, he never answers the door, the phone, or the mail. After all, monsters can be hiding anywhere. You can email his publisher Kissing Frog Books, and his editor will respond if she hasn't already been eaten. She'll let Tweedy know that his work has saved another reader from a cruel fate on the claws or in the jaws of a horrifying monster.

www.KissingFrogBooks.com

www.ingramcontent.com/pod-product-compliance
Lightning Source LLC
Chambersburg PA
CBHW031402040426
42444CB00005B/391